Turn Off The TV
Turn On Your Mind

Michele Doucette

Turn Off The TV: Turn On Your Mind

ISBN 978-0-9826302-0-4

Printed in the United States of America by

St. Clair Publications

PO Box 726

McMinnville, TN   37111-0726

http://stan.stclair.net

Table of Contents

Author's Note

The most beautiful thing we can experience is the mysterious. It is the source of all true art and all science. He to whom this emotion is a stranger, who can no longer pause to wonder and stand rapt in awe, is as good as dead; his eyes are closed.

These words attributed to Albert Einstein clearly show that, while an ingenious theoretical physicist, he was also a deep and astounding individual. We can learn much from these very words.

The cover image, *Le Penseur*, meaning *The Thinker*, readily captured what I was envisioning when writing this book. All credits are hereby given to Annelies Wienen for capturing such an outstanding photo.

To view more of her work, please take the time to visit http://www.flickr.com/photos/anneliesfotografeert/

In addition, I have to thank Kent Hesselbein, the cover design artist, for further blending this concept into something extraordinarily eye catching and intuitively symbolic.

I have just had the pleasure of reading the new book by Michele Doucette entitled *Turn Off The TV: Turn On Your Mind*, and found it very invigorating. I was immediately able to relate to the steps which Michele has taken to make her the knowledgeable and positive person that she is.

The book is not only replete with truisims, but contains many little-known Truths which have propelled enlightened individuals toward inner peace throughout the eons. The serious reader cannot help but deepen their Spiritual search by drinking in this work.

Cheers to Michele on a job well done!

– Stanley J. St. Clair, author of *Prayers of Prophets, Knights and Kings* and *Mysterious People of the Bible In The Light of History*

I've just read your book, and really enjoyed it. You cover so much material, it makes my head swim. Truth be told, I am simply amazed at where you find the time to read and write so prolifically. Although I haven't read anything on Gnosticism for years, your book draws me to explore that avenue. Eckhart Tolle's book, *A New Earth*, which I am just completing, has been the most eye opening.

While I've read various Buddhist texts relating to ego, Tolle's explanation of ego and how it works, and how to begin to overcome the habit of ego, and live in the now, is one of the most understandable I've read to date. If I were to have two books, I think I'd choose *Ancient Secrets of the Fountain of Youth*, which rites I am following now with good results, and *A New Earth*.

I really appreciate the fact that you are able to absorb and digest so much literature of a spiritual evolutionary nature, and pass along your thoughts and experiences to the rest of us. There is so much information out there. Having a glimpse of this material, with your synopsis, is a great help since we are on the same path; the path to awareness and self realization, the realization that our divinity lies within, as the source of all that is. May Spirit continue to guide you along your path.

– Susan Seaman, Canada

Another excellent read. I have to admit, the title struck me most, as it is what I strive to do. When I got into the "meat" of the book, I was happily surprised with more enlightening thoughts and ideas (other than simply turning off the TV). It was a very interesting and inspiring read.

Thanks, Michele for *another* great book.

– Genn Waite, owner/operator of Arkansas Crystal Works

I just finished reading your book and I was pleasantly surprised. Just like your other works, I thoroughly enjoyed the read. *Turn Off The TV: Turn On Your Mind* is filled with interesting ideas and spiritual principles. I love the simplicity of your writing. The *concepts are very easy to grasp*, yet *the wisdom they contain is profound*.

After reading your works, I can tell that not only do you believe that spirituality is meant to be simple, but you practice it. Thank you for putting this information out there.

– Jason Randhawa, WhatIsMetaphysics.com

Please do not be fooled by the title, *Turn Off The TV: Turn On Your Mind*, by thinking that this is a mundane book. This book is anything but that.

If you are just a beginner to spirituality, this book is offering a template for you to follow. If you think you have reached an intermediate level, this book can take you to a deeper understanding. If you believe that you are already an advanced entity, there are aspects of this book that will enable you to ponder, thereby assisting you further in your spiritual awakening.

From the opening statement, *To Be Or Not To Be*, Michele encourages you to contemplate the deeper meaning of To (Choose) To Be or To (Choose) Not To Be (Enlightened).

She then weaves concoctions of words and concepts that take you, the reader, to new depths in a clear, concise and easy manner, as well as offering numerable sources for you to research further, if that is your aspiration.

What is very obvious as one progresses into this book is that Michele expresses all of this material from her own experiences and her own understanding. I highly suggest this book to anyone on the Path of Enlightenment, declaring it is a *must* read.

– Elio Serra, USA

Absolutely superb are the first words that come to mind. I have read many, many things within the dreamstate reality and this work of yours is driving the message home.

You give *succinct explanations* to some rather perplexing areas, particularly about the nature of incarnation and what's going on inside our machine. You didn't fail to mention the ego and the power of illusion generated by that which is within everyone. You mentioned Jed McKenna, and how could you not? There are *so many links of helpful assistance* to anyone who has the thirst for knowledge concerning awareness.

There is one thing I am becoming more and more aware about and that is belief. Anything that needs, as a fundamental assumption, a belief as its basis is flawed. The reason is just this: in order to ascertain that, we need something tangible like a fact, but the truth is that nothing holds up under the light of truth. There is no real knowledge or certainty of anything except that we exist. So any belief, while it's certainly permissible to ponder such things, is just conjecture, a belief, a wisp of smoke.

I really love the way in which some ancient texts describe this: a silence; a stillness.

In that silence and stillness, however, words loose translation and meaning. This is the point where we no longer deny our existence, but embrace it in the only true capacity we can: *our own experience of existence*.

We live life no more in the meditative trance, not that kind of silence, but a stillness and silence that contains everything. The nothing that is ALL. *Everything is given to you because it comes forth from you and returns to you*.

I spend so much time trying to do what you're doing a superb job at, and that's describing this wondrous and radical paradigm shift. So many are doing this, it seems. How much better does it get?

We actually live in a beautiful arena of existence that the world has not been able to see. People are helping people and that's what you're doing Michele. How much more beautiful can you be? You are a blessing to so many.

– David Shirk, USA

I simply cannot keep up with Michèle's prolific output. I firmly believe Michèle is writing via divine guidance. Her work is *pertinent and useful* and will keep any searcher for truth going for a long time. Michèle is blessed by the gods with her *talent for writing*.

If anyone wants to contact me (lionjackie@aol.com) just in case they are skeptical, please do not hesitate.

– Jacqueline Lion, Certified Astrologist, Pendé, France

I like how your book begins with an explanation of duality along with a pointing toward nonduality and advice on how to pursue nonduality.

You then assert that the pursuit is dependent on an understanding of the mind, thereby *providing various ways to turn the mind toward its source*, toward the nondual, along with some interesting and practical diversions along the way.

The reader will learn how to realign the mind through affirmations, visualizations, gratitude, desire, and positive thoughts. Practical gains from proper mental positioning include health, money, love, and inner peace.

The purpose of this heightened mental awareness is *something deeper than the practical*, and you make that clear. The purpose of mental preparation is to make the pursuit of enlightenment feasible.

This book is *a fine guide and reminder for people who are wandering in the garden of spiritual and mental delights* and who intuit and need to pursue something deeper, known as source, God, soul, enlightenment, or nonduality.

Readers will be pleased to see serious reference to some well-known, and not so well-known names: Edgar Cayce, John Van Auken, Rev. Simeon Stefanidakis, Andrew Cohen and Eckhart Tolle, among others.

I also like the resource links denoted within the book, allowing the reader to expand the book at multiple points within the texts.

– Jerry Katz, author of *One: Essential Writings on Nonduality*

Rarely do I spend the additional funds to order a Pay Per View movie through my cable company, but the movie *Kite Runner* became available this week. I know the region and culture around Pakistan and Afghanistan fairly well and wanted to see this movie, fully expecting it would be trite and surface gloss only.

It has been 2 to 3 days since I saw the movie and my mind is still whirling and reeling from its impact for *it contained many lessons and connections which I also found you struggling to express in your book.*

On ego and ego-lessness, there is a critical scene in the movie where the main characters are children and best friends (and unknown to them, also half-brothers).

The older child would never "stick-up" for himself or others. The younger was always at the ready to defend his older friend.

One day the older boy witnessed the terrible beating and rape of the younger by town bullies. He hid and did nothing to interfere. The younger boy was badly beaten and traumatized but never said a word.

Soon after, the elder boy threw tomatoes at the younger, insulted him and begged him to strike back, but the younger boy would not.

Instead, he picked up a tomato and rubbed it into his own face as if to say "Here, I will help you dump your guilt on me. I love you too much to see you suffer even with this guilt. I am here for you to beat up on until you, too, understand the message and love me as I love you."

This act of total surrender of one's ego becomes the turning point for events later in their lives. It was the lesson given by a seven year old guru who understood, far better than anyone else, the true meaning of God and Love and selflessness. It was a life lesson about ego and non ego. For some, it comes naturally. For others, it must be learned and understood.

In the reading of your book I could see expressions of the same life lessons. I could also see the same expressions of selfless love. To find the words to express it so well to others is a true gift.

May God Bless You and help you to help others who share our journey.

– Suzanne Olsson, author of *Jesus In Kashmir, The Lost Tomb*

Foreword

To be, or not to be, that is the question.

Most are familiar with these words as taken from *Hamlet, Prince of Denmark*, written by William Shakespeare (1600). Interestingly enough, it may well be that Sir Francis Bacon, English philosopher, statesman, essayist, was the Stratford bard himself.

Knighted in 1603, Bacon was appointed to the position of Lord Chancellor by King James I of England, later attaining the position of official editor for the first authorized version of the King James Bible (1611). An aside note of delectable mystery appears to link Bacon to royal parentage, being an illegitimate son of Queen Elizabeth I and Robert Dudley, 1st Earl of Leicester.

The relevance of this particular line, *to be, or not to be*, strikes me as being one of the most valid spiritual comments that can be uttered within the current 21st century. However, its pertinence can only be applied to those who are willing to ask, and then answer, this very cryptic statement.

To Be or Not To Be

I am sure that many a mind has both wondered about, and debated over, the meaning of this rhetorical phrase. Truth be told, I had never given it much thought until now. It needs to be stressed, however, that in light of the time in which these words were composed, much was written in code.

To me, the words *to be, or not to be*, serve to highlight the duality of the cosmos, the inevitable existence of interconnected opposites: male and female, Yin and Yang, good and evil, day and night, life and death, happiness and sadness, new and old, spirit and body, same and different. Such is the harmony of two opposite, and, yet, complimentary parts that integrate into a whole. Such is the natural law that governs the whole of creation and life as we know it.

According to Rumi ... *No opposite can be known without its opposite. If duality did not exist, how would we know enough to yearn and strive for wholeness, for completion, for unity?*

There are also proponents who claim that duality means believing that we are alone, that we are isolated from others, that we are separate from All That Is.

It is my belief that all is connected, that all is one. In remembering our divine nature, we are both the whole and the parts of the whole; the interconnected totality of all life.

Such is where duality begins to blur, changing to nonduality.

This is where we begin to comprehend that we must strive to find the oneness, the unconditional love, the peace of mind, the true understanding, that exists beyond the duality of our experience.

Nonduality allows us to see that all is connected, that all is unified, that all shares a oneness. We are no longer separate. All that exists is in the here and now.

The question, then, becomes how do we get from here to there?

I chanced across a fellow Bluenoser (meaning someone who comes from Nova Scotia, Canada) when conducting research on the topic of non-duality. Jerry Katz is the author of *One: Essential Writings on Nonduality*.

In its compilation of the most lively expressions of non-duality, this tome greatly increases one's understanding. Herein, non-duality is explained from an impressive and diverse range of perspectives.

Katz also has a website dedicated to the subject, aptly called Nonduality: The Varieties of Expression [1] as well as a blog [2] for additional exploration. He also monitors a Nonduality Salon [3] yahoo email list. Katz also publishes a daily letter, Nonduality Highlights, [4] that one can read and subscribe to.

Katz states that "if you have ever had a sense of "something" deeper and more meaningful that lies beyond the everyday *you*, yet that *is* you in some way, you have had a taste of nonduality. The taste of nonduality is the sense of unity, peace, "something" vaster than the everyday you." [5]

---

[1] Katz, Jerry. *Nonduality: The Varieties of Expression* website located at http://www.nonduality.com/
[2] Katz, Jerry. *Nonduality Blog* located at http://nonduality.org/
[3] Katz, Jerry. *NondualitySalon* yahoo email list located at http://groups.yahoo.com/group/NondualitySalon/
[4] Katz, Jerry. *Nonduality Highlights* located at http://groups.yahoo.com/group/NDhighlights/
[5] Katz, Jerry. *Nonduality*. Retrieved April 27, 2008 from http://nonduality.net/

In continuation, "if you have ever felt deeply dis-satisfied, intensely unhappy, psychically imprisoned, it might be said that you can only feel this dis-satisfaction because part of you knows there is a place of freedom. That freedom is the experience of nonduality." [6]

What Katz shares next certainly resonated deeply within my soul.

"After experiencing the taste of nonduality, you may begin to *pursue* nonduality [through such mediums as books, crystals, meditation, teachers, spiritual practices, retreats] and since you are not separate from the "something" that is deeper, vaster, more meaningful than the everyday *you*, it follows that this pursuit is the *discovery of who you really are*." [7]

Clearly, I am learning that I am no stranger to nonduality at all, as this *is* my very pursuit. That having been said, I would never lay claim to being an expert, either.

---

[6] Katz, Jerry. *Nonduality*. Retrieved April 27, 2008 from http://nonduality.net/

[7] Ibid.

Despite the fact that there exists no scientific evidence to suggest that we use only 10% of our brains, I can only attest to my having believed this to be true.

In keeping, such meant that the remaining 90% of the brain was associated with untapped potential and unlimited possibilities.

Like a great many, I, too, have fallen into the New Age competition fray, wanting to further unlock the untapped hidden forces residing within my own mind, all courtesy of countless books, CDs and programs.

We are conditioned to believe that what we are looking for exists outside of ourselves. This is the belief that has served to help enslave us.

Truth be told, all that is needed to unlock the power of the human mind exists within, for the mind is incredibly dynamic and needs to be both recognized and acknowledged as such.

Learn deeply of the mind and its mystery for therein lies the true secret of immortality is the message put forth in *The Secret in the Bible.*

This sixteen-worded sentence "extracted from the ancient Book of God, a mysterious old document written on fabric of an unknown nature, and highly regarded by the Ancients thousands of years ago" [8] is what now serves to highlight my individual journey.

---

[8] Bushby, Tony (2003). *The Secret in The Bible* (p 6). Queensland, AU: Joshua Books.

The battlefield of the mind is merely the war that plays out between dark and light, a battle that everyone must conquer. Such is the journey of every human soul, the pathless journey towards self-realization, a journey in consciousness, a journey in metamorphosis. It is also the quest for self-transformation, the journey of an observer, the journey to freedom.

Such is the evolution of man. How, then, does one get there?

We have all experienced and lived the ego.

"The great enlightenment traditions have long spoken about the "enemy within" and about uprooting the need to cling to a false and separate sense of self. Their teachings encourage us to tame, transcend, purify – or in some cases slay – this pernicious foe of the spiritual heart." [9]

---

[9] What Is Enlightenment Magazine. (2008). *What is Ego? Friend or Foe.* Retrieved June 7, 2010 at http://www.enlightennext.org/magazine/j17/editorial.asp

It appears, however, that psychologists define ego from a different perspective, claiming it to be "the command center of the psyche without which we could not function. Not only is the ego essential to human development ... it is responsible for creating and sustaining the very civilization on which all of our lives depend." [10]

This previously cited editorial, then, puts forth a very important question.

What is the spiritual seeker to make of these two seemingly contradictory definitions?

This is, most definitely, a question to ponder, especially when "therapists tell us to develop the self" while the "Buddhists say there is no self." [11]

Taking it one step further, "psychologists explain how the ego is created" as compared with religions explaining "how the ego is transcended." [12]

---

[10] What Is Enlightenment Magazine. (2008). *What is Ego? Friend or Foe.* Retrieved June 7, 2010 at http://www.enlightennext.org/magazine/j17/editorial.asp
[11] Ibid.
[12] Ibid.

Andrew Cohen, dubbed the twenty-first century spiritual teacher and pioneer of evolutionary enlightenment, has come to understand that "the way in which we understand and relate to the ego has everything to do with the way in which we understand and relate to all life, including spiritual enlightenment." [13]

Clear as mud? Not really. However, continuing with this online website link will take you to several follow-up articles, all of which are quite illuminating.

What Is Ego? A Report from The Trenches [14]

When You Go Beyond the Ego You Become an Offering To The World [15]

The Enemy Within [16]

No Escape for the Ego [17]

---

[13] What Is Enlightenment Magazine. (2008). *What is Ego? Friend or Foe.* Retrieved June 7, 2010 at http://www.enlightennext.org/magazine/j17/editorial.asp
[14] http://www.enlightennext.org/magazine/j17/andrew.asp
[15] http://www.enlightennext.org/magazine/j17/amma.asp
[16] http://www.enlightennext.org/magazine/j17/dionysios.asp
[17] http://www.enlightennext.org/magazine/j17/sheng.asp

Yoga, Ego and Purification [18]

Is the Ego an Illusion? [19]

The Man with Two Heads [20]

The 1001 Forms of Self-Grasping [21]

The Transpersonal Ego: Is There A New Formation? [22]

Self-Acceptance or Ego-Death? [23]

Was ist "das Ich"? [24]

In keeping, Cohen further discloses insight into the two different parts of the self, one that is passionately interested in dynamic evolution (the Authentic Self [25]) and the other

---

[18] http://www.enlightennext.org/magazine/j17/desai.asp
[19] http://www.enlightennext.org/magazine/j17/bannanje.asp
[20] http://www.enlightennext.org/magazine/j17/frager.asp
[21] http://www.enlightennext.org/magazine/j17/engler.asp
[22] http://www.enlightennext.org/magazine/j17/puhakka.asp
[23]
http://www.enlightennext.org/magazine/j17/self_acceptance.
asp?page=1
[24] http://www.enlightennext.org/magazine/j17/wasist.asp
[25] Cohen, Andrew. (2009) Official Teacher of Spiritual Teacher and Founder of EnlightenNext magazine. *The Authentic Self: A Mysterious Compulsion to Evolve.*

which is deeply invested in its own narcissistic fears and desires (the Ego [26]) being the one and only obstacle to spiritual enlightenment.

One cannot be filled and directed by both darkness and light at the same time. There is a choice that must be made, with one of these facets taking over the helm of the mind.

Books have always played a role of major significance in my life, serving to enhance my own understanding of a great many diversified topics.

Eckhart Tolle has written several books that have propelled others forward, namely; *The Power of Now: A Guide to Spiritual Enlightenment* and *Practicing the Power of Now: Meditations, Exercises and Core Teachings For Living the Liberated Life*. His most current book, *The New Earth: Awakening to Your Life's Purpose*, is an absolutely phenomenal read.

Retrieved June 7, 2010 at
http://www.andrewcohen.org/teachings/authentic-self.asp
[26] Cohen, Andrew. (2009) Official Teacher of Spiritual Teacher and Founder of EnlightenNext magazine. *The Ego: An Anti-Evolutionary Force*. Retrieved June 7, 2010 at http://www.andrewcohen.org/teachings/ego.asp

The message of Eckhart Tolle is a very simple one: *living in the now is the truest path to enlightenment and happiness.* A first class teacher, Tolle has a way of writing with clarity and simplicity that one actually gets what he is trying to say.

Tolle has allowed me to see, with additional clarity, that my role, my purpose, involves being able to sense my essential Being-ness, the I AM, in the background of my life, at all times and in all situations. It is so simple and yet so utterly profound. This, then, becomes my own personal ascension.

Not everyone will be ready for Jed McKenna and the books that make up The Enlightenment Trilogy. [27]

In *Spiritual Enlightenment: The Damnedest Thing*, McKenna carefully distinguishes religiosity from mystical experience, neither having anything to do with enlightenment, which merely equates to abiding nondual awareness, meaning *no self.* McKenna states that the only way to get to enlightenment comes down to *continually* searching out what is true.

Writing within his own experience from the nothingness of the Void, McKenna's lean, mean and tough stance challenges anyone with a belief system.

---

[27] http://www.wisefoolpress.com/

Spiritually Incorrect Enlightenment, the second book in the trilogy, is a book about injunction, compelling an individual to refrain from thinking and engaging in the same old way, thereby invoking a negation process in the nondual tradition. As the reader will by now have surmised, McKenna's approach to enlightenment and awakening is anything but orthodox.

We finish the trilogy off with *Spiritual Warfare* wherein we are invited to fight in a war like no other – a war where loss is counted as gain, a war where surrender is counted as victory, a war where the enemy you must face, an enemy of unimaginable superiority, is none other than yourself.

I hereby challenge you to challenge yourself.

Negative feelings, thoughts and emotions are like toxins, that, if suppressed and/or held onto for long periods of time, will manifest in physical form. This is why it is important to learn how to release negativity.

Learning how to change negative self-talk into positive self-talk takes time, especially considering the fact that we are only consciously aware of approximately 10% of the thoughts that buzz and chatter about in our heads.

For many years, too numerous to count, I found myself constantly in a state of worry, stress, fear and guilt, both at home and in the workplace.

Watching the news on TV kept me in a controlled state of restless anxiety. I had no idea that the media was so biased in their news coverage, that it was their job to saturate us, to have everyone view the news in the same way, thereby responding in kind.

This meant that there was great propensity for millions and millions of people to broadcast similarly negative responses.

Like a sponge, when surrounded by like-minded people, I would sink deeper and deeper into depressive states. I was being controlled by that voice in my head.

It was impossible to achieve a positive outlook on life when my mindset was one of negativity.

As soon as I became aware that thoughts, words, actions and emotions were energy based, I knew that I had no choice but to reconfigure the wiring of my brain.

I had to learn to think and respond from a more positive outlook. I was no longer willing to allow my ego to reign supreme.

How does one begin to go about understanding how they think?

How does one begin to examine, without criticism, the belief system(s) that they are privy to?

The easiest way to start is by *observing your actions and reactions* to people, to things, to situations, in your physical world.

In addition, and as much as possible, you must also learn to *detach from subjectivity.*

Remaining as objective as is possible, your goal becomes understanding *why* you think the thoughts that you do and *why* you respond to people and situations in a specific way.

Once you begin questioning your 'programmed' beliefs and ideas, you need to be ready to replace them with beliefs and ideas that *resonate with you*. In so doing, you begin to embark on an internal and personal mental shift.

Do not be afraid to seek the answers to questions that all individuals, at some time, ask of themselves.

Who am I? Why am I here? What is my purpose? What is reality?

Do not be afraid to question the information that comes to you.

As you begin questioning, thereby experiencing this much needed and necessary internal shift, your energy signature, your vibration, changes.

You will find yourself aligning, more and more, with a higher consciousness. This is what is meant by the *thinning of the veil*.

An individual journey of Gnosis, such was the beginning of my trek: to release my mind from the dream.

While there are countless websites to be discovered by each and every one, so that they, too, can begin their Gnostic journey, here are a few to sample and explore.

Gnostic Judas [28]

Early Christian Writings – Gnostics, Gnostic Gospels and Gnosticism [29]

Essene Blessing Walk One [30]

Essene Blessing Walk Two [31]

Essene Healing Breath Introduction [32]

Essene Healing Breath Phase One [33]

Essene Healing Breath Phase Two [34]

Essene Healing Breath Phase Three [35]

---

[28] http://www.gnosticjudas.com/
[29] http://earlychristianwritings.com/gnostics.html
[30] http://modernessenes.com/walk/index.html
[31] http://modernessenes.com/walk/five.html
[32] http://www.modernessenes.com/breath/index.html
[33] http://modernessenes.com/apprentice/one-b.html
[34] http://modernessenes.com/apprentice/two-b.html
[35] http://modernessenes.com/apprentice/three-b.html

Turn Off The TV

Universal Gnostic Fellowship [36]

Gnostic Lessons [37]

In working with thought forms, stay positive. It is only in thinking positive thoughts that we continue to attract more positive people and positive events/happenings into our lives. In this way we become like the ripples in the pond, creating a domino of positive effects out into the world.

On the flip side, the more we focus on the negative, the depressed, the dismal ... the more negativity we bring into our lives.

Clearly, we must become more aware of our thoughts in order to eliminate the unnecessary negative or judgmental ones.

It is for this very reason that I no longer watch the news on TV, read magazines or listen to the radio. I have eliminated all media negativity in my life for the simple reason that I was finding myself existing in a state of distress, unable to focus on the wondrous joys associated with life and living.

---

[36] http://gnosticfellowship.com/
[37] http://www.gnosticlessons.com/about.html

In keeping with the changes that we are trying to bring forth within, it is important to remember that for every action or non-action, there is a consequence.

When we give our minds and our responsibility away, we give our lives away. Is this what we want?

It is important to become aware that most of the media is controlled by just a few. *Take the time to use discernment.*

Look for the hidden agenda, as summarized here in bullet form, courtesy of David Icke.

• *Why* is this information being presented to you?

• What is their *real* agenda?

• Is it a case of problem-reaction-solution?

• Do *they* create a problem so that *we* react and ask for a fix?

• Do *they* then offer a solution?

• Is the *solution* what *they* really wanted in the first place?

The real power lies with the many, not the few. Do not allow yourself to be fooled.

Infinite power exists within every individual.

We have the power to decide our own destiny, but *only* if we do not give that power away.

When something happens that we do not like, we often look for someone else to blame. When there is a global problem in the world, we often wonder what *they* are going to do about it.

It is exactly this form of non-action that has resulted in the giving away of significant individual power.

The few want to control your mind because, when they have succeeded in doing that, they have you.

This is why *the answer lies in taking the mind back*, in thinking for ourselves and allowing others to do the same, without condemnation or ridicule.

We create our own reality by our thoughts and our actions. If we change our thoughts and actions, we *can* change the world. This is where all individual transitioning must begin.

Everyone lives in the world of his or her thoughts. As stated before, thoughts are energy; hence, positive thoughts attract positive results, naturally, while negative thoughts attract negative results.

In short, like attracts like. All vibration seeks its own level.

Interestingly, "body parts, including cells and organs, have *vibratory signatures*," [38] be they healthy or diseased. It is in "understanding these scientifically, and having the advanced technology to alter our bodies' vibrational signatures that allows us to heal many ailments." [39]

Let's face it, we tend to hang around people who are like us, people who think the way we think.

Our thoughts, beliefs, expectations, words and actions create a magnetic field around us that attracts people and situations that match our energy and our vibration.

We attract those things in our life (money, relationships, employment) that we focus on. Even though it is not as simple as stating an affirmation, no affirmation is going to work if your mind (thought) is negating the positive.

When we focus on having less, this is exactly what we create for ourselves.

In this regard, you must *know what you want*.

------

[38] *Chapter 19: The Children of The Law of One Basic Meta-Physics of Science-Magic* article. Retrieved June 7, 2010 from http://www.atlantis.to/LTA/chapter-nineteen-pg7.htm
[39] Ibid.

Monitor your thoughts carefully, being sure to only think about what you want, because the universe will take a snapshot of your thoughts for manifestation purposes.

Make what you want your burning desire, your major purpose, for it will be these very thoughts that shall manifest in form.

Remain determined to see them fully realized, for success comes to those who have success consciousness.

You get what you think about, what you focus on, what you talk about and what you believe.

Ultimately, it is a belief system based on thought and action.

To become peace in action, one must be peace.

To become love in action, one must be love.

To become forgiveness in action, one must be forgiveness.

Everything is the result of mere thought. It is *the mind* that *is the builder towards a caring, unselfish and harmless world.*

Affirmations, positive self talk and visualizations are easily counted among the different methods that have been utilized as powerful ways of programming your mind in preparation for success consciousness.

Affirmations are personal statements written in both positive and present tense terms. *The more emotion one provokes* upon saying these affirmations aloud, *the more powerful they become.*

Affirmations are positive statements, or directions, you make to yourself in order to bring about changes in your subconscious behavior patterns to whatever you will them to be.

"Using an affirmation is like planting a seed in the fertile soil of your sub-conscious mind, and like a seed it needs daily tending or it will die. For this reason, affirmations are tools that are used daily, and frequently, by those who wish to change." [40]

For affirmations to be effective, they must always be stated as positive, already accomplished, results.

----

[40] Peniel, Jon. (1997). *The Children of the Law of One and The Lost Teachings of Atlantis* (p. 249). Alamosa, CO: Network.

Wording them in futuristic terms, such as [1] **I will be,** [2] **I am going to be, [3] I would like to be** actually *prevents the changes from ever taking place* because we are always in the now.

In addition, *giving energy to the positive trait* (**I am always Unselfishly Loving**) always *supercedes the negative* (**I will become Unselfishly Loving**).

You need to both *feel, believe* and *mean* the words as you say them, or the affirmation will not be an effective tool.

Creating a visual image to accompany your words is also important. Some people like to create a type of "wish" board whereby they collect an assortment of pictures and/or photographs to represent what they are creating.

When it comes to visualization, I find it incredibly difficult to both see the pictures and try to put myself in the image. I find it extraordinarily difficult to get emotionally excited about these impressions when all my mind sees are some dark and fuzzy attempts at a new reality. Now that I have discovered Mind Movies, [41] an absolutely phenomenal metaphysical tool, this no longer presents a problem.

---

[41] http://www.mindmovies.com/?10107

In all honesty, it really does not matter if you cannot visualize very well, as long as you know how to watch videos.

Likewise, it really does not matter if you cannot raise your emotional vibration easily, as long as you like music.

Mind Movies is a *multi-media tool* that allows you to create a vision of what you want, scored with your favorite song; the one that makes you feel good, the one that makes you want to dance, the one that makes you smile and sing along.

Mind Movies has allowed me make my *dreams* and *desires* a monumental part of what I *see* and *hear* every day.

Watching the Mind Movie every morning and every evening helps in manifesting through the Law of Attraction. In fact, I was able to manifest a brand new laptop using this method; the very one that has created this manuscript.

Gratitude for every aspect of your life that is, and is yet to come, *is one of the keys* to the secret of the Law of Attraction.

Too often in our busy lives we forget to be grateful for what we have.

Take the time to stop and appreciate.

Be thankful for your health, for life, for your achievements, for the beauty and wonder of nature, for everyone and everything that contributes to this magnificent and miraculous journey.

Give gratitude. Feel gratitude.

As you become truly appreciative for everything in your life, including those things yet to arrive, you will be truly amazed at how much the feeling of gratitude opens the floodgates of the universe to bring more to you.

More people are waking up to the fact that, in making these necessary and needed thought changes, they are allowing their own frequencies to assist others in this much needed planetary change.

In this sense, these changes can be seen as a true act of co-creation whereby Heaven is coming to earth and earth is rising up to Heaven, meaning that it is not just a top down frequency raising, it is also a raising upward, which is a true melding of humanity and divinity.

How To Create Positive Coincidences [42]

----

[42] http://evolutionezine.com/positive-coincidences/

Turn Off The TV

Send Negative Energy Packing [43]

Take Control of Your Subconscious Mind [44]

The Creation Game [45]

The Prosperity Game [46] (was first introduced by Abraham and Esther Hicks, the teachers of *Deliberate Creation*)

Validation: Award Winning Short Film [47]

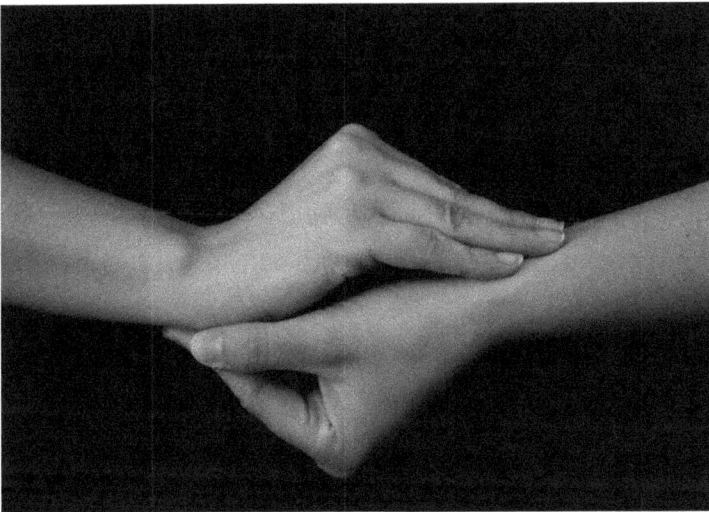

Perfect Balance Mudra

---

[43] http://evolutionezine.com/positive-energy/
[44] http://evolutionezine.com/subconscious-mind/
[45] http://evolutionezine.com/this-is-your-creation/
[46] http://www.choosingprosperity.com/game/
[47] http://evolutionezine.com/will-make-you-smile/

What do we call that part of us that is always connected to the Source, even when we are unsure? I grew up thinking that the words soul and spirit meant that same thing, that they could be used interchangeably. There are also many others who believe the two to be one and the same.

The writings of Edgar Cayce show that he was able to discern a clear distinction between spirit and soul. While "Spirit is the spark, or portion, of the Divine that is in every entity," [48] he also believed it to be a consciousness, reflected within the one, universal, collective mind of God.

It is the Spirit self that was created in the image of God, as recorded in Genesis 1:26. This is that part of us that seems to correspond with the biblical passage, *You are gods, sons of the Most High* (Psalm 82).

---

[48] Van Auken, John. (2002). *Understanding Soul and Spirit* article. Retrieved June 7, 2010 from Edgar Cayce's Association for Research and Enlightenment, Inc. website located at
http://www.edgarcayce.org/ps2/soul_life_soul_spirit.html

Van Auken shares that Cayce saw the soul as being that which is "ever changing, growing, and learning" while using "free will to explore, create, test, discover." [49]

Cayce also believed the soul to be "the ultimate companion to the Creator, a true companion, because it has the free will to choose to be a companion or not." [50]

In addition, it is the soul that is able to "bridge the gulf between the spirit realms and the physical realms, between our divine, godly self and our earthly self." [51]

It is the *mind* of the soul, that which psychologists have referred to as our subconscious, however, that "may operate independently of the Collective Consciousness of the Creator." [52]

Many wish to re-attune with the Source. This seems to be what Eastern seekers refer to as entering the Void.

---

[49] Van Auken, John. (2002). *Understanding Soul and Spirit* article. Retrieved June 7, 2010 from Edgar Cayce's Association for Research and Enlightenment, Inc. website located at
http://www.edgarcayce.org/ps2/soul_life_soul_spirit.html

[50] Ibid.
[51] Ibid.
[52] Ibid.

How, then, is one able to accomplish this merging with the *All That Is*, you ask?

Stuart Dean, the manager of A.R.E.'s Study Group department, had an experience whereby he was able to feel the difference between spirit and soul.

He stated that "as Spirits, we are eternally young, perfect, innocent, and happy. Creative energies before creation, with feelings of perfect willingness to cooperate with every other spirit, knowing that we are all units of One Love." [53]

In keeping, he talked about how *childlike and unafraid* these spirits are. Could it be that these very attributes might hold an important key?

Van Auken believes there to be a distinctive difference between the spirit and the soul. "The soul is on a journey with many twists and turns in the road of life. But the spirit is high above the road, overarching it from beginning to end, and knows the peace that passes understanding, the

---

[53] Van Auken, John. (2002). *Understanding Soul and Spirit* article. Retrieved June 7, 2010 from Edgar Cayce's Association for Research and Enlightenment, Inc. website located at
http://www.edgarcayce.org/ps2/soul_life_soul_spirit.html

contentment that is never shaken, the Paradise that is ours to enjoy forever." [54]

In reference to traditional Christianity, I grew up believing in the Trinity: the triune aspect of Father, Son/Daughter and Holy Spirit. In continuation, my experience of Catholicism placed considerable emphasis on God, both a deity as well as a human image.

However, "there is a more fundamental truth deeply inherent within most religious and spiritual pathways – God is spirit. If God is One, there can be no splitting of God into gender, form, or any other physical or spiritual personage." [55]

In keeping, "as Spirit, we were created and we live in God's image of Spirit. Thus, within us, we have all the attributes

---

[54] Van Auken, John. (2002). *Understanding Soul and Spirit* article. Retrieved June 7, 2010 from Edgar Cayce's Association for Research and Enlightenment, Inc. website located at http://www.edgarcayce.org/ps2/soul_life_soul_spirit.html
[55] Stefanidakis, Rev. Simeon. (2001). *Helping Understand the Mystery of Spirit-Soul-Body* article. Retrieved June 7, 2010 from First Spiritual Temple website located at http://www.fst.org/trinity.htm

of God, we are all part of God and of God's Spirit, and we are created of the same stuff as God, but we are not God." [56]

Stefanidakis continues further by saying that "your Spirit is that part of you which is the direct creation of God. Your spirit is devoid of all elements of human personality and character." [57]

Clearly, these explanations, as offered by Stefanidakis, seem to be in alignment with the teachings of Edgar Cayce.

In continuance, "the Spirit is one with all and understands, fully, that oneness, as well as its oneness with God, its Creator." [58]

Furthermore, "there are no evil spirits. The most heinous people to have walked the earth were created in the very same image as were the saints. On that level of life ... there is only Spirit." [59]

---

[56] Stefanidakis, Rev. Simeon. (2001). *Helping Understand the Mystery of Spirit-Soul-Body* article. Retrieved June 7, 2010 from First Spiritual Temple website located at http://www.fst.org/trinity.htm
[57] Ibid.
[58] Ibid.
[59] Ibid.

As perfect a copy as we are, will this always be the distinction between us, the Creation, and God, the Creator?

Now comes the interesting part.

"Just as God created us in *His* image, as Spirit; in order for us to live the Human experience, *we* created an image in the likeness of our Spirit," [60] This image is the Soul.

Is this what is meant by our being called co-creators with God?

"Your Soul is that part of your Spirit which has human character and which links with the human experience." [61]

Let us recap what has been stated, thus far.

Your Soul is an image of your Spirit.

Your Spirit is an image of God.

"It is the Soul which "descends" from the home of the Spirit and resides within a level of Creation somewhat removed (in

---

[60] Stefanidakis, Rev. Simeon. (2001). *Helping Understand the Mystery of Spirit-Soul-Body* article. Retrieved June 7, 2010 from First Spiritual Temple website located at http://www.fst.org/trinity.htm
[61] Ibid.

terms of vibration) from that of the Spirit," remembering that "the Soul is closely linked to the Earth plane and the human experience." [62]

It is the Soul that is sometimes referred to as one's Higher Self, that "part of us which guides, through intuition and through its connection with the Spirit and with God, our earthly affairs." [63]

It is important to remember that it is the Soul that is evolving, courtesy of many earthly incarnations. It is equally important to remember that the Soul is directly connected with human personality and character.

Given its various personality manifestations while here on the earth plane, we do experience limitation at the Soul level.

While there are no evil Souls, according to Stefanidakis, there are *less good* Souls. To further explain, he shares that "within the home of the Soul, spirituality is measured and made manifest not by the comparison of goodness and evil,

---

[62] Stefanidakis, Rev. Simeon. (2001). *Helping Understand the Mystery of Spirit-Soul-Body* article. Retrieved June 7, 2010 from First Spiritual Temple website located at http://www.fst.org/trinity.htm
[63] Ibid.

but by the various degrees of goodness manifested within the multitude of soul lives." [64]

To continue, "the Soul evolves, through choice and karma, ever guided by the Spirit which, in turn, is ever guided by God. In many ways, the Soul is the *prodigal son* seeking to return to the Father." [65]

In order for the Soul to incarnate, there has to be a physical body. This is how the creation of the Personality [also identified as the Psyche] comes into being, courtesy of a physical vehicle.

I am of the complete acceptance that we have lived within multiple bodies at various times throughout the course of history (reincarnation).

It is in so doing that each time a Soul makes a conscious decision to incarnate, a new earthly personality is created along with the necessary physical body.

---

[64] Stefanidakis, Rev. Simeon. (2001). *Helping Understand the Mystery of Spirit-Soul-Body* article. Retrieved June 7, 2010 from First Spiritual Temple website located at http://www.fst.org/trinity.htm
[65] Ibid.

All of us are able to identify with the personality through components such as gender, form, race, social standing, ethnic attributes.

All are born into a specific family (genetics) with a specific name. Although our spiritual bodies are comprised of energy and light, it is not so with the personality born into the physical body.

In forgetting who and what we really are, we have a tendency to believe that the physical, along with the personality, is key.

It is the *Personality* living on the Earth plane that becomes "susceptible and receptive to negativity and evil," [66] a very real force unto itself, "created and made manifest by the various people who inhabit the earth." [67]

This means that "somewhere, between the level of the Soul and the level of the Personality – somewhere between the

---

[66] Stefanidakis, Rev. Simeon. (2001). *Helping Understand the Mystery of Spirit-Soul-Body* article. Retrieved June 7, 2010 from First Spiritual Temple website located at http://www.fst.org/trinity.htm
[67] Ibid.

second and third elements of the trinity – there can be created and made manifest evil and negativity." [68]

In summation, as per Stefanidakis .....

• your Spirit is always guided by God

• your Soul is always guided by your Spirit

• your Soul always seeks to guide you and your Personality in the daily affairs of your life

• your Personality can choose to accept or decline this guidance (consciously or otherwise)

This is the Trinity of Spirit–Soul–Body/Personality of which Stefanidakis speaks.

From a more esoteric perspective, I prefer to relate to this trinity model.

"No matter who we are, where we may be, or what we are experiencing, God's Guiding Light is always there and freely offered." [69]

---

[68] Stefanidakis, Rev. Simeon. (2001). *Helping Understand the Mystery of Spirit-Soul-Body* article. Retrieved June 7, 2010 from First Spiritual Temple website located at http://www.fst.org/trinity.htm

"Spiritual evolution is the process whereby the earthly Personality is elevated and brought into *at-one-ment* with the Soul, while the Soul is elevated and brought into *at-one-ment* with the Spirit," with death being "the returning of the Personality back to the Soul, bringing into the essence of the Soul all that it learned and experienced, both positive and negative, here on the Earth plane." [70]

This has to be one of the most eloquent versions of spiritual evolution that I have ever come across.

To continue, "the Soul, guided by the Spirit and by God's Holy Spirit, then decides how it will make manifest the lessons it has received from the Personality, as well as make amends, through the Great Law of Karma, for the injustices it may have committed against others, against God, and against itself ... through *successive incarnations* until it reaches a point where the earthly Personality is a perfect

---

[69] Stefanidakis, Rev. Simeon. (2001). *Helping Understand the Mystery of Spirit-Soul-Body* article. Retrieved June 7, 2010 from First Spiritual Temple website located at http://www.fst.org/trinity.htm
[70] Ibid.

manifestation of the Soul's goodness," [71] on earth as it is in Heaven, as the saying goes.

How wondrous to know that at this point one's Soul no longer needs to incarnate, thereby moving along in its evolution back to Spirit.

Here are some additional websites for exploring.

The Nature of Soul [72]

The Senses of Soul [73]

The Heart of Soul [74]

The Characteristics of Soul [75]

The Sound of Soul [76]

---

[71] Stefanidakis, Rev. Simeon. (2001). *Helping Understand the Mystery of Spirit-Soul-Body* article. Retrieved June 7, 2010 from First Spiritual Temple website located at http://www.fst.org/trinity.htm
[72] http://www.soulandspirit.org/natureofsoul.htm
[73] http://www.soulandspirit.org/sensesofsoul.htm
[74] http://www.soulandspirit.org/heartofsoul.htm
[75] http://www.soulandspirit.org/characteristicsofsoul.htm
[76] http://www.soulandspirit.org/soundofsoul.htm

Turn Off The TV

The Spirit of Soul [77]

The Mystical Experience Registry: Body, Soul and Spirit Awareness [78]

The Mystical Experience Registry: Body Defined [79]

The Mystical Experience Registry: Soul Defined [80]

The Mystical Experience Registry: Spirit Defined [81]

---

[77] http://www.soulandspirit.org/spiritofsoul.htm

[78]

http://www.bodysoulandspirit.net/bodysoulandspirit/define/index.shtml

[79]

http://www.bodysoulandspirit.net/bodysoulandspirit/define/bodydefined.shtml

[80]

http://www.bodysoulandspirit.net/bodysoulandspirit/define/souldefined.shtml

[81]

http://www.bodysoulandspirit.net/bodysoulandspirit/define/spiritdefined.shtml

Rosicrucian Triad of Body, Soul and Spirit [82]

Soul Transformation [83]

Spiritual Quest

---

[82] http://www.kheper.net/topics/Anthroposophy/Steiner-levels_of_self.htm

[83]

http://newconnexion.net/articles/index.cfm/2003/07/zaviska.html

The spiritual exercise of attention is the same as (1) existing in the now, (2) living in the zone, and (3) the practicing of mindfulness. While thusly engaged, you are able to acknowledge that this is the only time when you are really living. Mindfulness allows us to make any activity and/or exercise a spiritual activity. This is exactly what I attempt to focus on, as I strive to go about my business each and every day.

"The exercise of attention is exercising and developing consciousness of awareness itself. And, for every situation we can exercise attention in, it is another situation where we are now free not only to act, but to be. This is not only a basic skill and a place to start on the path to Gnosis, it is a very powerful tool in its own right, for it is the ability to focus, to shine, the light within." [84]

---

[84] Pierce, Rev. Troy W. (2007). *Following The Path of Gnosis: The Spiritual Exercise of Attention* article. Retrieved June 7, 2010 from http://gnoscast.blogspot.com/2008/03/following-path-of-gnosis-spiritual.html

There is a book called *Cognitive Models and Spiritual Maps* (ISBN 0907845134), a reprint of the November/December 2000 issue of the Journal of Consciousness Studies, that talks about a variety of scientific fields (cognitive science, neuropsychology, developmental psychology, philosophy of the mind, anthropology) that have joined together to further investigate the phenomenon of consciousness.

Although it is "a mistake to simply equate Gnosis with enlightenment," [85] it can be said that "Gnosis is the method (means) of liberation" [86] as opposed to the liberated state itself. Gnosis is "a way to refer to a fundamental spiritual growth, transformation, liberation process." [87]

For those that wish to explore religious traditions as well as the Gnostic tradition, please visit the Gnosis Institute [88] whereby they share the following.

---

[85] Pierce, Rev. Troy W. (2007). *Questions: Practices for Gnosis* article. Retrieved June 7, 2010 from http://gnoscast.blogspot.com/2008/02/questions-practices-for-gnosis.html
[86] Ibid.
[87] Ibid.
[88] The Gnosis Institute. (2008) Retrieved April 27, 2008 at http://gnosisinst.org/

"Gnosis is not what you think. It is not an idea, not a doctrine. It is not objective. It is not definable. It is not found inside of rigid limits, not outside of all considerations. It is not yours. It is not ours. It is something attained, and is a quickening of what we already have. It is a knowledge that you *are*, not a knowledge that you *have*.

"If you are looking for a label, Gnosis is not it. If you are seeking a path with answers, Gnosis is not it. If you are looking for a path that fits you, Gnosis is not it. If you are seeking what is real beyond yourself and your ideas, then you may already be on the path of Gnosis.

"We do not seek to propagate a set of beliefs or doctrines, nor to spread one set of teachings or one perspective. We seek to follow the injunction from the Gospel of St. Thomas – *If you see what is before your face, there is nothing that will not be revealed to you.* We seek to know what is real, and to follow that beyond our current notions, ideas, and understandings. We stand apart from mainstream culture only in that we do not prejudice the real to exclude the spiritual. We do not exclude what has always been a part of human experience, what has always been a part of human culture. For to do that would be to veer from the path of Gnosis towards mere ideas.

"Gnosis is not what you think. And it is not something you will understand quickly. It is something you will come to know, and grow in that knowing.

"Scriptures tell us that the truth shall make us free. In Greek, the word for *truth* is "un-hidden". The un-hidden, the unveiled, the examined shall set us free. This requires discipline and commitment, training and work. It requires an allegiance to the real that is higher than the allegiance to the ideal.

"How seriously do you take your spiritual path? How committed are you to your liberation?"

If this message resonates with you, please take the time to check out the Gnosis Institute (as per the previous link).

In the earliest of my research, I was under the impression that Gnosis was the Greek word for *knowledge*.

I have since discovered that there are three essential Classical Greek words that speak to different types of knowledge: doxia, episteme, gnosis, all of which Rev. Troy

W. Pierce further discusses in his blog article entitled *Gnosis, Episteme, and Doxia, Oh My!* [89]

The path of Gnosis is an individual one. This clearly means that *my path is my responsibility*. For those who strongly adhere to a culture of collective religious identity, this concept is not easily understood.

"From the perspective of the Gnostic tradition, personal growth and transformation is what it is all about, expressed as Gnosis – a very deep and sure knowing, a knowing that you are, rather than a knowing that you possess. It is a true knowing that is liberating. Gnosis is this way of knowing, and with it comes a deep understanding of who we are, and where we are, and what sets us free." [90]

I have recently discovered a website called **I**magination **A**wakened **M**insitry, denoted also as **I AM**, whereby mankind is awakening into a new era.

---

[89] Pierce, Rev. Troy W. (2007). *Gnosis, Episteme, and Doxia, Oh My!* article. Retrieved June 7, 2010 from http://gnoscast.blogspot.com/2007/11/gnosis-episteme-and-doxia-oh-my.html
[90] Pierce, Rev. Troy W. (2007). *Questions: Approaching Gnosticism* article. Retrieved June 7, 2010 from http://gnoscast.blogspot.com/2007/08/questions-approaching-gnosticism.html

"The Human Mind is the vehicle in which consciousness enters into and experiences creation. One aspect of the mind is Thought ... the other is Imagination, which is its natural evolution. Thought and Imagination are two sides of the same coin." [91]

In essence, one's imagination creates one's experience. One's world is an expression of their wonderful human imagination. We become what we think.

Might it be that we can learn to understand thought enough to create something new for ourselves? Imagination allows one to live in the "freedom of limitless possibility, for all things in this world are imagination of which consciousness is the animating power in a world of shadows. It has been said that God is in all things." [92] Imagination, ergo, is God. To God, all things are possible. Hence, it can be said that the same is reflective of Imagination.

One attracts what they believe to be true. This is why it is *so* important to *become aware of your unconscious programming*, your unconscious patterns.

––––––––––––––––––––

[91] *Universal Laws* article located on the Imagination Awakened Ministry website. Retrieved June 7, 2010 from http://www.i-am.cc/us/Ministry.htm
[92] Ibid.

In so doing, you become even more aware of the world around you, including the belief systems of others.

Clearly it is time to become more aware of the world that exists within, one that has been freed from the egoic mind.

I applaud the creators of the **I AM** site, in that they refer to themselves as *Ministers of Imagination* and *Midwives of Human Consciousness*.

The only cure for evil, suffering, and all problems that we are faced with in today's world lies in losing 'separate consciousness' and selfishness by regaining consciousness of our oneness with everything.

This can only be attained through unselfish love, looking to both Jesus and Buddha as important and living examples of what is representative of true spirituality: compassion, kindness, caring, giving, sharing and harmlessness.

We must see the illusions of self consciousness that we carry with us in our mind and break them.

I see this as being a very exciting time. In knowing that we create our own reality by the very thoughts that we think, the very words that we verbalize, the very actions that we employ, now is the time to learn to let go of fear and concentrate solely on the expansion of love and forgiveness.

In talking about Body, Mind and Spirit, I think that I have finally been able to grasp the distinctive differences that exist.

Being the avid reader, researcher, and writer that I am, books have always been one way for me to explore and integrate new information.

In so doing, I always take what resonates, from any engaged text, leaving the rest behind.

Very much a believer in synchronicity, books and websites just seem to appear when I begin actively looking for something specific.

In keeping with the topic of Soul, Spirit and Personality, I was drawn to an online Spiritual Soul Journey program, as taught by Andrew Schneider.

It is Schenider himself who shares that "the foundation of the New Spirituality is intelligent understanding" and that "through understanding, love and empowerment become real. With understanding comes transformation." [93]

The *New Spirituality*. Hmmmmm. I rather like that term. In keeping with my own journey, I have a tendency to borrow a little from here and a little from there, putting it all together into something that holds true for me at any given moment in time. In this regard, the *New Spirituality* is a term that seems to work for me.

While I have yet to explore the site more thoroughly, I am resonating deeply with my newest discovery.

There are 4 levels to the Soul Journey program.

Level 1: Know Yourself: Understand Soul, Spirit and Personality [94]

The seeker will delve into the world of Spirit, Soul and Personality. One will then be provided with new perspectives on understanding how personality interacts with soul.

---

[93] Robson, John. (2008). *The Soul Journey* article. Retrieved May 7, 2008 from http://www.thesouljourney.com/spiritual-journey.shtml
[94] http://www.thesouljourney.com/what-is-soul.shtml

Level 2: Develop and Heal the Personality [95]

The seeker will be introduced to understanding how the building of personality development leads the way to soul consciousness.

Level 3: Developing and Expressing Soul Consciousness [96]

The seeker will be introduced to the four levels of soul relationship contact (within ourselves, with each other, with the whole world, with the Universe/God).

Level 4: Discover Your Soul Purpose [97]

The seeker will learn that they have *three* life purposes: a personality purpose, a soul purpose and a Spirit purpose.

In addition, they also offer an online Spiritual Counseling Course [98] wherein the seeker will learn how to help others on their soul journey.

---

[95] http://www.thesouljourney.com/personality-development.shtml
[96] http://www.thesouljourney.com/spiritual-growth.shtml
[97] http://www.thesouljourney.com/soul-purpose.shtml
[98] http://www.thesouljourney.com/spiritual-counseling-course.shtml

Andrew Schneider offers additional ebooks well worth exploring; namely,

Spiritual Alchemy: The Alchemist's Dream [99]

Authentic Living [100]

Overcoming Life's Challenges [101]

The Years Leading Up To 2012 [102]

In addition, he also offers Spiritual Retreats and Classes in British Columbia, Canada.

In continuation, most of humanity identifies fully with the ego, believing that this is who they really are, releasing oneself from the egoic mind is a difficult task.

The most daunting challenge that all have to face is this: we are *not* our thoughts and emotions.

---

[99] http://www.thesouljourney.com/spiritual-alchemy.shtml
[100] http://www.thesouljourney.com/authenticity.shtml
[101] http://www.thesouljourney.com/life-challenges.shtml
[102] http://www.thesouljourney.com/years-2009-2008-2012.shtml

Turn Off The TV

Although I am unsure as to where the term *egoic mind* originated, it is so-called, and most aptly, due to the fact that as long as one identifies with the 'thinker', there is a sense of self (the ego) connected to every thought, every memory, every opinion, every viewpoint, every interpretation, every reaction, and every emotion.

The function of the egoic mind is to maintain control, thereby keeping one prisoner in the linear and logical mind. As the egoic mind surrenders, we begin to engage in a more conscious experience.

Once there, much vigilance is needed, initially, in order to maintain the stillness. The more you are able to remain within the silence, the chattering of the mind continues to lessen.

Until the egoic mind has dissolved completely, one must continue to be alert to its subterfuge, whether in yourself and/or others. This is a process that has taken me years.

If this sounds rather intimidating, it need not be; humor is a most valuable tool that can be used to short-circuit the spell of the egoic mind.

Upon succeeding, one is able to both experience and acknowledge authentic power as being completely different from ego based power.

I quickly came to realize that I was here to be of service (my family, my students, my friends, Mother Earth), but all without taking away from myself.

Edgar Cayce likens the death of the ego to "the symbology behind the crucifixion of Christ." [103]

The best thing that we can do to save the world is to save the world from our own righteousness as "it is our righteous egoic mind which makes us see problems. In Truth, the only problem is the prevailing mentality that problems do exist and our projection of them into each other and the world. This is actually the most essential message spiritual masters and enlightenment teachers have been sharing with us throughout the ages." [104]

Nebot continues by sharing that "by being conscious of our triggers, reactions and projections we can transcend them. As we transform, our world transforms. So before becoming an activist to fight for whatever cause you consider noble,

---

[103] Williams, Kevin. (2006). *Edgar Cayce on Human Origins* article. Retrieved June 7, 2010 from http://www.near-death.com/experiences/cayce03.html
[104] Nebot, Jesus. *How to save the world from yourself* article. Retrieved June 7, 2010 from http://www.ru.org/personal-development/how-to-save-the-world-from-yourself.html

consider first that, perhaps, the only thing wrong with the world is your perception of it." [105]

As you "start releasing all the opinions, beliefs, emotions and perceptions that are keeping you separated from others, from this world, and ultimately from God ... you will realize that, in Truth, we are all One. You will be blessed with full understanding, acceptance and compassion for everyone and everything. You may still feel inspired to take action, but it won't be motivated by judgment, fear, greed, blame, need, moral obligation or any other egoic energy that motivates most people. Instead, your actions will be inspired by pure, unconditional Love for all that exists. A Divine Love that will take over your life and guide you to selflessly serve other people, animals, nature and the planet at large. Then the world will be saved because you will be saved." [106]

[105] Nebot, Jesus. *How to save the world from yourself* article. Retrieved June 7, 2010 from http://www.ru.org/personal-development/how-to-save-the-world-from-yourself.html
[106] Ibid.

What is enlightenment? This seems to be the multi-million dollar question of the 21st century.

To answer, enlightenment is what you make of it.

One starts by respecting the living spirit that is at work in their life – be it a walk in the rain, an aerobic workout, reading a book, making a meal, or washing the dishes.

As you continue to grow, courtesy of the path you have chosen, you will realize that your course will change as you change.

Every individual, advancing on his/her own path, will, at some point, experience an individualized enlightened state.

Yod He Vau He [107] the most ancient name for the Universal Spirit, being "the physical word equivalent of a vibrational, or thought form" [108] was not meant to be an actual name.

---

[107] *Chapter 19: The Children of The Law of One Basic Meta-Physics of Science-Magic* article. Retrieved June 7, 2010 from http://www.atlantis.to/LTA/chapter-nineteen-pg15.htm

"Contained in this one name for the One, is the actual formula for creation, and the manifestation of all life within the one. Thus this name of God is probably the single, most significant and metaphysical term there is." [109]

This most ancient name is "represented by four letters in what is now called the Hebrew alphabet, which have numerical, as well as symbolic, meanings." [110]   For those who may not know, Yod He Vau He is pronounced Yohd-Hay-Vah-Hay. [111]

"The ancient teachings say that 'He who can pronounce this name properly opens the gates of heaven'," [112]   primarily because "in the early days of 'religion', certain 'priests' or high priests in power positions, who wanted more power, didn't want the common people to know this great key. They wanted people to *need* to go to the priests and turn to the religion for their understanding of God and spiritual

---

[108] *Chapter 19: The Children of The Law of One Basic Meta-Physics of Science-Magic* article. Retrieved June 7, 2010 from http://www.atlantis.to/LTA/chapter-nineteen-pg15.htm
[109] Ibid.
[110] Ibid.
[111] Ibid.
[112] *Chapter 19: The Children of The Law of One Basic Meta-Physics of Science-Magic* article. Retrieved June 7, 2010 from http://www.atlantis.to/LTA/chapter-nineteen-pg16.htm

matters. This gave them great power and control, so they hid the name, changed the name or made it forbidden to say by anyone other than the 'high holy people'." [113]

"The symbolism and structure of Yod-He-Vau-He is simple, yet deeply profound. And when its few simple elements combine, they give birth to the entire complexity of life. In part, YHVH represents that perfect simple pattern ... the atom or solar system. It also speaks of human procreation, and stellar/planetary procreation." [114]

"The first part, "Yod", represents the positive (+), "Sun", "light", "the Father" principles." [115]

"The first part "He", represents the negative, not in the sense of "bad" or "evil", but in the sense of negative (-) polarity, pure darkness like that of the void of space, the receptive, the Mother principles." [116]

In continuation, "Vau" is the meeting of Yod and He – the place of interplay, intercourse, and combining of the first

---

[113] *Chapter 19: The Children of The Law of One Basic Meta-Physics of Science-Magic* article. Retrieved June 7, 2010 from http://www.atlantis.to/LTA/chapter-nineteen-pg16.htm
[114] Ibid.
[115] Ibid.
[116] Ibid.

two principles.   It is its own principle, and the place of
conception of, and the birth of, the second "He" (again,
pronounced "hay")." [117]

By comparison, "the second "He" is the offspring of Yod
and He, the result of their interaction, their subsequent
creation. The second "He" has the same attributes as its
Father, the Yod, in that it actually IS a Yod in its own macro
or microcosmic realm. The second "He" is on a vibrational
plane an octave apart." [118]

"The second "He" begins the cycle (Yod-He-Vau-He) again,
but AS THE YOD in micro-cosm or macro-cosm, and its
polarity is reversed from its "father" Yod. Interestingly, the
"father" principle, Yod, was distorted through translation
over time from "Yod" into "God", which is also often given
a "father" principle connotation." [119]

---

[117] *Chapter 19: The Children of The Law of One Basic Meta-Physics of Science-Magic* article. Retrieved June 7, 2010 from http://www.atlantis.to/LTA/chapter-nineteen-pg16.htm
[118] Ibid.
[119] Ibid.

If you go to page 17 [120] of this continued online text, you can read more about how the cycle of YVHV creation continues as an Infinite spiral.

"YVHV's most important representation is *the means of transition and manifestation of creation infinitely throughout all.* If one truly understands YVHV, one understands the Law governing all vibration and all creation." [121]

---

[120] *Chapter 19: The Children of The Law of One Basic Meta-Physics of Science-Magic* article. Retrieved June 7, 2010 from http://www.atlantis.to/LTA/chapter-nineteen-pg17.htm

[121] *Chapter 19: The Children of The Law of One Basic Meta-Physics of Science-Magic* article. Retrieved June 7, 2010 from http://www.atlantis.to/LTA/chapter-nineteen-pg18.htm

In returning to *learn deeply of the mind and its mystery for therein lies the true secret of immortality*, the message put forth in *The Secret in the Bible* as shared on page 18, it seems timely to also position the same message here.

While the success of the egoic mind causes sure death to the physical body, resulting in the continued existence of the universal incarnation cycle, achieved enlightenment is akin to the attaining of immortality, due to the fact that the cosmic life cycle of birth and death for the soul ceases to exist.

The moment one reaches a state of nothingness, the countdown has already begun!

What better reason do you need to pursue enlightenment?

The End

I do not foresee the end as being the literal end.

In retrospect, what is an ending, if not a new and unforeseen beginning?

As written by Gary Crowley in *From Here To Here: Turning Toward Enlightenment*.

"Awakening to enlightenment is a journey from here to here, not from here to there. There is nowhere to go and nothing to be attained. Enlightenment is simply an awakening to what has always been the case." [122]

I wish you much joy in the journey, as you also make your way to the peaceable kingdom within. Clearly, in order to do so, you must, as the title so aptly puts it, *Turn Off The TV* in order to *Turn On Your Mind*.

Make it your intention to ascend.

---

[122] Crowley, Gary. (2006). *From Here to Here: Turning Toward Enlightenment* (p 3). Boulder, CO: GL Design.

Bibliography

Braden, Gregg. (1995) *Awakening to Zero Point: The Collective Initiation.*

Braden, Gregg. (1997) *Walking Between the Worlds: The Science of Compassion.*

Braden, Gregg. (2000) *The Isaiah Effect: Decoding the Lost Science of Prayer and Prophecy.*

Braden, Gregg. (2000) *Beyond Zero Point: The Journey to Compassion.*

Braden, Gregg. (2004) *The God Code: The Secret of Our Past, The Promise of Our Future.*

Braden, Gregg. (2004) *The Divine Name: Sounds of the God Code.* (Audio Book)

Braden, Gregg. (2005) *The Lost Mode of Prayer.* (Audio CD)

Braden, Gregg. (2005) *Unleashing The Power of The God Code: The Mystery and Meaning of the Message in Our Cells.* (Audio CD)

Braden, Gregg. (2005) *An Ancient Magical Prayer: Insights from the Dead Sea Scrolls*. (Audio Book)

Braden, Gregg. (2005) *Speaking the Lost Language of God: Awakening the Forgotten Wisdom of Prayer, Prophecy and the Dead Sea Scrolls*. (Audio Book)

Braden, Gregg. (2005) *Awakening the Power of A Modern God: Unlock the Mystery and Healing of Your Spiritual DNA*. (Audio Book)

Braden, Gregg. (2006) *Secrets of The Lost Mode of Prayer*.

Braden, Gregg. (2007) *The Divine Matrix: Bridging Time, Space, Miracles and Belief*.

Breathnach, Sarah Ban. (1996) *Simple Abundance: A Daybook of Comfort and Joy*.

Breathnach, Sarah Ban. (2000) *The Simple Abundance Companion: Following Your Authentic Path To Something More*.

Brezny, Rob. (2005). *Pronoia Is The Antidote For Paranoia: How The Whole World Is Conspiring To Shower You With Blessings*.

Bunick, Nick. (1998) *In God's Truth*.

Bunick, Nick. (2010) *Time for Truth: A New Beginning*.

Chopra, Deepak. (1998) *The Path to Love: Spiritual Strategies for Healing*.

Chopra, Deepak. (2005) *Peace Is The Way: Bringing War and Violence to An End*.

Coelho, Paulo. (1998) *The Alchemist*.

Coelho, Paulo. (2004) *Warrior of The Light: A Manual*.

Das, Lama Surys. (1998) *Awakening the Buddha Within*.

Das, Lama Surys. (2000) *Awakening to the Sacred: Creating a Spiritual Life From Scratch*.

Das, Lama Surys. (2001) *Awakening the Buddhist Heart: Integrating Love, Meaning and Connection into Every Part of Your Life*.

Das, Lama Surys. (2003) *Living Kindness: The Buddha's Ten Guiding Principles for a Blessed Life*.

Das, Lama Surys. (2003) *Letting Go of the Person You Used To Be: Lessons on Change, Loss and Spiritual Transformation*.

Doucette, Michele. (2010) *A Travel in Time to Grand Pré* (second edition).

Doucette, Michele. (2010) *The Ultimate Enlightenment For 2012: All We Need Is Ourselves.*

Dyer, Wayne. (1998) *Manifest Your Destiny: The Nine Spiritual Principles For Getting Everything That You Want.*

Dyer, Wayne. (2002) *Getting in the Gap: Making Conscious Contact with God Through Meditation.* (Book and CD)

Gawain, Shakti. (1993) *Living In The Light: A Guide to Personal and Planetary Transformation.*

Gawain, Shakti. (1999) *The Four Levels of Healing.*

Gawain, Shakti. (2000) *The Path of Transformation: How Healing Ourselves Can Change The World.*

Gawain, Shakti. (2003) *Reflections in The Light: Daily Thoughts and Affirmations.*

Gelb, Michael. (2005) *Da Vinci Decoded.*

Hansard, Christopher. (2003) *The Tibetan Art of Positive Thinking.*

Hicks, Esther and Hicks, Jerry. (2004) *Ask and It Is Given: Learning to Manifest Your Desires*.

Hicks, Esther and Hicks, Jerry. (2004) *The Teachings of Abraham: Well-Being Cards*.

Hicks, Esther and Hicks, Jerry. (2005) *The Amazing Power of Deliberate Intent: Living the Art of Allowing*.

Hicks, Esther and Hicks, Jerry. (2008) *The Astonishing Power of Emotions: Let Your Feelings Be Your Guide*.

Hicks, Esther and Hicks, Jerry. (2009) *The Vortex: Where the Law of Attraction Assembles All Cooperative Relationships*.

Kelder, Peter. (1998) *Ancient Secret of the Fountain of Youth, Book 1*.

Kelder, Peter. (1998) *Ancient Secret of the Fountain of Youth, Book 2*.

Kelder, Peter. (2008) *The Eye of Revelation: The Ancient Tibetan Rites of Rejuvenation*.

Koven, Jean-Claude. (2004) *Going Deeper: How To Make Sense of Your Life When Your Life Makes No Sense*.

Lama, Dalai. (2004) *The Wisdom of Forgiveness: Intimate Conversations and Journey*.

Millman, Dan. (2000) *Way of the Peaceful Warrior*.

Millman, Dan. (1991) *Sacred Journey of the Peaceful Warrior*.

Millman, Dan. (1992) *No ordinary Moments: A Peaceful Warrior's Guide to Daily Life*.

Millman, Dan. (1995) The *Life You Were Born To Live*.

Millman, Dan. (1999) *Everyday Enlightenment*.

Morgan, Marlo. (1995) *Mutant Message Down Under*

Morgan, Marlo. (1998) *Mutant Messages From Forever: A Novel of Aboriginal Wisdom*.

Nichols, L. Joseph. (2000) *The Soul As Heaker: Lessons in Affirmation, Visualization and Inner Power*.

Peniel, Jon. (1998) *The Lost Teachings of Atlantis: The Children of The Law of One*.

Peniel, Jon. (1999) *The Golden Rule Workbook: A Manual for the New Millennium*.

Price, John Randolph. (1987) *The Superbeings.*

Price, John Randolph. (1998) *The Success Book.*

Quinn, Gary. (2003) *Experience Your Greatness: Give Yourself Permission To Live.* (Audio CD)

Redfield, James. (1995) *The Celestine Prophecy.*

Redfield, James. (1998) *The Tenth Insight.*

Redfield, James. (1997) *The Celestine Vision: Living the New Spiritual Awareness.*

Redfield, James. (1999) *The Secret of Shambhala.*

Renard, Gary. (2004) *The Disappearance of the Universe.*

Renard, Gary. (2006) *Your Immortal Reality: How To Break the Cycle of Birth and Death.*

Ruiz, Don Miguel. (1997) *The Four Agreements: A Practical Guide to Personal Freedom.*

Ruiz, Don Miguel. (1999) *The Mastery of Love: A Practical Guide to The Art of Relationship.*

Ruiz, Don Miguel. (2000) *The Four Agreements Companion Book.*

Ruiz, Don Miguel. (2004) *The Voice of Knowledge: A Practical Guide to Inner Peace*.

Ruiz, Don Miguel. (2009) *The Fifth Agreement: A Practical Guide to Self-Mastery*.

Schuman, Helen. (1997) *A Course in Miracles*.

Shinn, Florence Scovel. (1989) *The Wisdom of Florence Scovel Shinn*.

Shinn, Florence Scovel. (1991) *The Game of Life Affirmation and Inspiration Cards: Positive Words For A Positive Life*.

Shinn, Florence Scovel. (2006) *The Game of Life*. (Book and CD)

Tolle, Eckhart. (2004) *The Power of Now: A Guide to Spiritual Enlightenment*.

Tolle, Eckhart. (2001) *Practicing the Power of Now: Meditations, Exercises and Core Teachings for Living the Liberated Life*.

Tolle, Eckhart. (2003) *Stillness Speaks*.

Tolle, Eckhart. (2005) *A New Earth: Awakening to Your Life's Purpose*.

Tolle, Eckhart. (2001) *The Realization of Being: A Guide to Experiencing Your True Identity*. (Audio CD)

Tolle, Eckhart. (2003) *Entering The Now*. (Audio CD)

Twyman, James. (1998) *Emissary of Peace: A Vision of Light*.

Twyman, James. (2000) *The Secret of the Beloved Disciple*.

Twyman, James. (2000) *Portrait of the Master*.

Twyman, James. (2000) *Praying Peace*.

Twyman, James. (2008) *The Moses Code: The Most Powerful Manifestation Tool in the History of the World*.

Twyman, James. (2009) *The Kabbalah Code: A True Adventure*.

Twyman, James. (2009) *The Proof: A 40-Day Program For Embodying Oneness*.

Vanzant, Iyanla. (2000) *Until Today*.

Virtue, Doreen. (1997) *The Lightworker's Way*.

Virtue, Doreen. (2006) *Divine Magic: The Seven Sacred Secrets of Manifestation*. (Book and CD)

Walker, Ethan III. (2003) *The Mystic Christ: The Light of Non-Duality and the Path of Love According to the Life and Teachings of Jesus.*

Walsch, Neale Donald. (2002) *The New Revelations: A Conversation with God.*

Walsch, Neale Donald. (2000) *Bringers of The Light.*

Walsch, Neale Donald. (1999) *Abundance and Right Livelihood: Applications for Living.*

Walters, J. Donald. (2000) *Awaken to Superconsciousness: How To Use Meditation for Inner Peace, Intuitive Guidance and Greater Awareness.*

Walters, J. Donald. (2000) *Meditations to Awaken Superconsciousness: Guided Meditations on The Light.* (Audio Cassette)

Walters, J. Donald. (2003) *Meditation for Starters.* (Book and CD)

Walters, J. Donald. (2003) *Metaphysical Meditations.* (Audio CD)

Walters, J. Donald. (2003) *Secrets of Bringing Peace On Earth.*

Weiss, Brian. (2001) *Messages From the Masters: Tapping Into The Power of Love.*

Weiss, Brian. (2002) *Meditation: Achieving Inner Peace and Tranquility in Your Life.*

Williamson, Marianne. (1996) *A Return To Love.*

Williamson, Marianne. (1997) *Morning and Evening Meditations and Prayers.*

Williamson, Marianne. (2002) *Everyday Grace: Having Hope, Finding Forgiveness and Making Miracles.*

Williamson, Marianne. (2003) *Being In Light.* (Audio CD set)

Yogananda, Paramahansa. (1979) *Metaphysical Meditations: Universal Prayers, Affirmations and Visualizations.*

Zukav, Gary. (1998) *The Seat of The Soul.*

Zukav, Gary and Francis, Linda. (2001) *The Heart of The Soul: Emotional Awareness.*

Zukav, Gary and Francis, Linda. (2003) *The Mind of The Soul: Responsible Choice.*

Zukav, Gary and Francis, Linda. (2003) *Self-Empowerment Journal: A Companion to The Mind of The Soul: Responsible Choice.*

Zukav, Gary. (2007) *Soul To Soul: Communications from the Heart.*

Zukav, Gary. (2010) *Spiritual Partnership: The Journey to Authentic Power.*

About the Author

Michele Doucette is webmistress of Portals of Spirit, a spirituality site whereby one will find links to (1) an ezine called Gateway To The Soul, (2) books of spiritual resonance, (3) categories of interest from Angels to Zen, (4) Soulutions, (5) up-to-date information as shared by a Quantum Healer, (6) healing resource advertisements and (7) spiritual news.

In addition, she holds a Crystal Healing Practitioner diploma (Stonebridge College in the UK). As a Level 2 Reiki Practitioner, she sends long distance Reiki to those who make the request, claiming only to be a channeler of the Universal Energy, thereby allowing the individual(s) in question to heal themselves.

Love ~ Peace ~ Freedom

www.ingramcontent.com/pod-product-compliance
Lightning Source LLC
Chambersburg PA
CBHW070546030426
42337CB00016B/2365